GALE
CENGAGE Learning

Literature of Developing Nations for Students, Volume 1

Staff

Series Editors: Elizabeth Bellalouna, Michael L. LaBlanc, and Ira Mark Milne.

Contributing Editors: Elizabeth Bodenmiller, Reginald Carlton, Anne Marie Hacht, Jennifer Smith.

Managing Editor: Dwayne Hayes.

Research: Victoria B. Cariappa, *Research Team Manager*. Maureen Eremic, Barb McNeil, Cheryl Warnock, *Research Specialists*. Andy Malonis, *Technical Training Specialist*. Barbara Leevy, Tamara Nott, Tracie A. Richardson, Robert Whaley, *Research Associates*. Scott Floyd, Nicodemus Ford, Sarah Genik, Timothy Lehnerer, *Research Assistants*.

Permissions: Maria Franklin, *Permissions*

Manager. Margaret A. Chamberlain, Edna Hedblad, *Permissions Specialists.* Erin Bealmear, Shalice Shah-Caldwell, Sarah Tomasek, *Permissions Associates.* Debra Freitas, Julie Juengling, Mark Plaza, *Permissions Assistants.*

Manufacturing: Mary Beth Trimper, *Manager, Composition and Electronic Prepress.* Evi Seoud, *Assistant Manager, Composition Purchasing and Electronic Prepress.* Stacy Melson, *Buyer.*

Imaging and Multimedia Content Team: Randy Bassett, *Image Database Supervisor.* Robert Duncan, Dan Newell, *Imaging Specialists.* Pamela A. Reed, *Imaging Coordinator.* Dean Dauphinais, Robyn V. Young, *Senior Image Editors.* Kelly A. Quin, *Image Editor.*

Product Design Team: Kenn Zorn, *Product Design Manager.* Pamela A. E. Galbreath, *Senior Art Director.* Michael Logusz, *Graphic Artist.*

Library of Congress Cataloging-in-Publication Data

Literature of developing nations for students / Michael L. LaBlanc, Elizabeth Bellalouna, Ira Mark Milne, editors.

v.; cm.

Includes bibliographical references and index.

Contents: v. 1. A-L — v. 2. M-Z.

ISBN 0-7876-4928-7 (set: alk. paper) — ISBN 0-7876-4929-5 (vol. 1) — ISBN 0-7876-4930-9 (vol. 2)

1. Fiction—Stories, plots, *etc.* 2. Fiction—History and criticism. 3. Developing countries—Literatures

—History and criticism. [1. Fiction—Stories, plots, *etc.* 2. Fiction—History and criticism. 3. Developing countries—Literatures—History and criticism.] I. LaBlanc, Michael L. II. Bellalouna, Elizabeth. III. Milne, Ira Mark. IV. Title.
PN3326 .L58 2000
809'.891724—dc21
00-056023

Copyright Notice

Copyright © 2000
Gale Group, Inc.
27500 Drake Road
Farmington Hills, MI 48331-3535

ISBN 0-7876-4929-5

Printed in the United States of America.

10 9 8 7 6 5 4 3 2 1

The Farming of Bones

Edwidge Danticat

1998

Introduction

The Farming of Bones, Danticat told Megan Rooney in *The Brown Daily Herald,* is a survivor's story, based on the true story of a woman who was killed in the massacre. "But I wanted her to live," Danticat says, and in the book, she does. The book, which has received almost universally favorable reviews, is based on historical facts, filtered through Haitian tales and oral history, "a collage of various characters and experiences from my upbringing in

Haiti," she told Rooney.

Although Danticat was still in her twenties when her first book, *Breath, Eyes, Memory,* was published, it received critical acclaim and was selected for Oprah Winfrey's book club, rocketing it to the top of the bestseller lists and commercial success. This success eventually led Penguin to pay $200,000 for the paperback rights to *The Farming of Bones.*

Danticat spent several years researching the events in *The Farming of Bones,* traveling to Haiti as many as four times a year. After visiting the Massacre River there in 1995, she realized that she wanted to write a book about the 1937 massacre of Haitians by Dominican dictator Rafael Trujillo. When she visited, there was no sign of the mass killings that occurred so many decades ago: a woman was washing clothes in the water, a man was letting a mule drink, and two boys were bathing. The river itself was small and slow, nowhere near the high-water mark that once swallowed hundreds of bodies. "I had come looking for deaths," she wrote in *Kreyol,* "but I found habitualness, routine, life."

Despite this peace, or perhaps because of it—because the event and the people who suffered in it seemed to have been lost and forgotten—she decided to memorialize them by writing the book. "I felt like I was standing on top of a huge mass grave, and just couldn't see the bodies," she told Mallay Charters in *Publishers Weekly,* and reflected, "It's part of our history as Haitians, but it's also a part of the history of the world. Writing about it is an act of remembrance."

Danticat does not merely write about Haiti, but is still active in the Haitian community. With writer Junot Diaz, she runs Haitian-Dominican youth groups in New York, and also works with the National Coalition for Human Rights as part of a grant from the Lila Wallace-Readers Digest Foundation.

Author Biography

Edwidge Danticat (pronounced "Edweedj Danticah") was born January 19, 1969, in Port-au-Prince, Haiti, and was separated from her father when she was two and he emigrated to the United States to find work. When she was four, her mother also went to the United States. For the next eight years, Danticat and her younger brother Eliab were raised by their father's brother, a minister, who lived with his wife and grandson in a poor section of Port-au-Prince known as Bel Air.

When Danticat was twelve, she moved to Brooklyn and joined her parents and two new younger brothers. Adjustment to this new family was difficult, and she also had difficulty adjusting at school, because she spoke only Creole and did not know any English. Other students taunted her as a Haitian "boat person," or refugee. She told Mallay Charters in *Publishers Weekly,* "My primary feeling the whole first year was one of loss. Loss of my childhood, and of the people I'd left behind—and also of being lost. It was like being a baby—learning everything for the first time."

Danticat learned to tell stories from her aunt's grandmother in Bel Air, an old woman whose long hair, with coins braided into it, fascinated the neighborhood children, who fought each other to comb it. When people gathered, she told folktales and family stories. "It was call-and-response,"

Danticat told Charters. "If the audience seemed bored, the story would speed up, and if they were participating, a song would go in. The whole interaction was exciting to me. These cross-generational exchanges didn't happen often, because children were supposed to respect their elders. But when you were telling stories, it was more equal, and fun."

Danticat's cousin, Marie Micheline, taught her to read. She told Renee H. Shea in *Belles Lettres,* "I started school when I was three, and she would read to me when I came home. In 1987…there was a shooting outside her house—where her children were. She had a seizure and died. Since I was away from her, my parents didn't tell me right away…But around that same time, I was having nightmares; somehow I knew."

When Danticat was seven, she wrote stories with a Haitian heroine. For her, writing was not a casual undertaking. "At the time that I started thinking about writing," she told Calvin Wilson in the *Kansas City Star,* "a lot of people who were in jail were writers. They were journalists, they were novelists, and many of them were killed or 'disappeared.' It was a very scary thing to think about." Nevertheless, she kept writing. After she moved to Brooklyn and learned English, she wrote stories for her high school newspaper. One of these articles, about her reunion with her mother at age twelve, eventually expanded to become the book *Breath, Eyes, Memory.*

Danticat graduated from Barnard College with

a degree in French literature in 1990, and worked as a secretary, doing her writing after work in the office. She applied to business schools and creative writing programs. She was accepted by both, but chose Brown University's creative writing program, which offered her a full scholarship. For her master's thesis, she wrote what would later become *Breath, Eyes, Memory*.

Breath, Eyes, Memory and her two other books —*The Farming of Bones* and *Krik? Krak!*, a collection of stories—have been hailed for their lyrical intensity, vivid descriptions of Haitian places and people, and honest depictions of fear and pain.

Danticat has won a Granta Regional Award as one of the Twenty Best Young American Novelists, a Pushcart Prize, and fiction awards from *Seventeen* and *Essence* magazines. She is also the recipient of an ongoing grant from the Lila Wallace-Reader's Digest Foundation.

After her parents drown in the flooded Massacre River that marks the border between Haiti and the Dominican Republic, young Haitian Amabelle Desir becomes a housemaid to Dominican landowner Don Ignacio, and a companion to his daughter, Valencia. As the book opens, Valencia and Amabelle are grown women, and Amabelle attends the birth of Valencia's twins. Valencia is now married to a Dominican army officer seeking to rise in the ranks, and he is soon assigned to assist in the brutal slaughter of Haitians in the Dominican Republic.

Amabelle's lover, Sebastien, works in Ignacio's sugar cane field, a brutal job known to workers as "farming the bones" because of its killing, exhausting harshness.

Amabelle has a pleasant but distant relationship with the family she serves, and the novel juxtaposes her moments in their home with her conversations with other Haitian workers in the cane fields, as they slowly realize that Dominican dictator Trujillo is against them, and that their lives are worthless to those who hire them. This tension increases when a cane worker is accidentally killed by Duarte's poor driving, and he is not brought to account for the murder; no one, other than the Haitians, seems to care.

When the roundup and killing of Haitians

begins, Sebastien disappears, presumably killed. Amabelle manages to escape, fleeing toward Haiti over mountain trails. Many others, also escaped, are pursued, forced to jump off cliffs, beheaded, or beaten to death before they ever cross the border into Haiti. The Dominicans identify Haitians by language, since despite the fact that Dominican propaganda states that Dominican origins are in Spain and the Haitians' are "in darkest Africa," there are no color differences between the two groups—the only difference is that the Haitians cannot pronounce the r *in perejil,* the Spanish word for "parsley." Some of the refugees in the book, in fact, are Dominicans who were attacked or killed because at first sight they appeared to be Haitian, and even Valencia's twins show this racial mix— one is dark, the other light, though they both grew in the same womb.

The most perilous part of Amabelle's journey back to Haiti occurs in Dajabon, the Dominican town closest to the Massacre River, which marks the border between the two countries. She and other refugees are herded together, attacked, and choked with parsley, while the Dominican attackers demand that they say "perejil." Because their language is Creole, not Spanish, they are unable to pronounce it correctly, and some are choked to death on handfuls of the herb; people throw stones at them, attack them with machetes, and brutally punch and kick them. She and some others escape only because the crowd is distracted by the arrival of the Dominican dictator, Trujillo, and they flee toward the river.

The river is filled with the corpses of slaughtered Haitians, and soldiers are throwing more bodies off a nearby bridge. As they swim across, one of the other refugees is shot, and his wife panics. Amabelle, in an attempt to keep her quiet and thus prevent the soldiers from noticing them and killing them too, covers the woman's nose and mouth with her hands. Although Amabelle does not intend to kill her, the woman dies.

Amabelle goes home with Yves, another refugee, and lives with him as if they are married, but is never intimate with him: she is still grieving for Sebastien. She finds Sebastien's mother's house and talks to her, but his mother soon moves to a distant city, because she can no longer bear talking to people who tell her that her son is dead.

In the wake of the massacre, the government sends officials to pay off surviving family members and to hear the stories of survivors. Amabelle and Yves go to the city to tell their stories, and after they wait for several days, they are turned away. They later find out that they will not receive any compensation after all. Danticat describes the scene: "The group charged the station looking for someone to write their names in a book, and take their story —they wanted a civilian face to concede that what they had witnessed and lived through did truly happen."

Much later, Amabelle, still seeking answers to her questions about why this all happened and what happened to Sebastien, crossed the river again and returns to Alegria, the Dominican region where she used to live. But the familiar landmarks are gone, she is disoriented and confused, and even Valencia has moved to a new house and does not recognize her at first. Eventually, she finds the cave she used to meet Sebastien in, but there are no answers there. At the end of the book she returns to the river, still seeking answers; as the book ends, she is lying in the current, giving herself up to fate and the forward flow, with faith for a new life.

Characters

Amabelle Desir

Amabelle is orphaned at a young age when her parents drown in the river between Haiti and the Dominican Republic, as they try to cross over to attend a market on the far side. Distraught, she tries to follow them, but two river-crossing guides hold her back, saying, "Unless you want to die, you will never see those people again." She is found on the riverbank by kindhearted and wealthy landowner Don Ignacio, who asks her, "Who do you belong to?" "To myself," she answers. He takes her in as a house servant, where she grows up with his daughter Valencia; as Valencia grows up, Amabelle becomes her personal maid, altering the relationship from personal companion to respectful servant. When Valencia has twins and there is no one else to attend her unexpected and early delivery, Amabelle serves as midwife, having picked up a smattering of knowledge about this from her parents, who were both traditional healers back in Haiti.

Alone and alienated, a stranger in a strange land, Amabelle clings to her lover Sebastien, who works at brutally hard labor in the sugar cane fields. They meet often in a secret cave behind a waterfall, and she says of him, "When he's not there, I'm afraid I know no one and no one knows me." Having taken the place of her family, he is her rock in life. Like her, he has suffered loss—his father was killed in a hurricane—and their shared sadness bonds them together.

When Dominican dictator Rafael Trujillo begins a genocidal campaign against all Haitians in his country, Amabelle must flee for her life. She is a survivor at all costs: determined, driven, she will do whatever it takes to live. When, in the ensuing chaos, Sebastien disappears and is presumed killed, she must once again rely on her own instincts.

Amabelle makes it across the border to Haiti, but not without paying a heavy price in physical and emotional suffering. For many years afterward, she grieves for Sebastien, even going back to the Dominican Republic in an attempt to find their old secret cave. Driven to find answers to the questions that haunt her—why people suffer, why they die, why she lived when others perished—she returns to the river, hoping "that if I came to the river on the right day, at the right hour, the surface of the water might provide the answer...But nature has no memory."

Don Ignacio

A wealthy Dominican landowner, Valencia's father, and employer of Amabelle and Sebastien. He was born in Spain, and constantly looks back to his lost homeland. Each night he listens to the radio for broadcasts of the progress of the Spanish Civil War. As Amabelle notes, "He felt himself the orphaned child of a now orphaned people." Sympathetic to the suffering of others, he takes Amabelle into his household when he finds her orphaned on the riverbank; this sympathy comes from the fact that although he is wealthy now, his background was humble. Back in Spain, he says, "My father was a baker…There are times when he gave bread to everyone in our quarter for nothing. I was his only son but he would never let me eat until everyone else had eaten." When his son kills a Haitian worker with his car, Don Ignacio is sympathetic and wants to visit the grieving father, but he is human and has limits—when his own grandson dies, he forgets all about this, wrapped up in his own pain.

Doctor Javier

An intense, educated man, he admires Amabelle's intelligence and determination and invites her to work in a clinic in Haiti with him when he finds out that her parents were healers and that she has successfully midwifed Valencia's twins. "You can be trained," he says. "We have only two Haitian doctors for a large area. I cannot go there all the time, and I know of only one or two midwives in that region of the border. You are greatly needed." When he hears about the genocide, he warns Amabelle and others to run and tells her he and others have room in their trucks for her, but before this happens, he is arrested and is never seen again.

Kongo

An old mask maker and carpenter, whose true name is unknown. His son is struck and killed by Pico Duarte's car. When the genocide begins, he tells Amabelle that she must escape. He does not try to escape, saying that he is too old to run, but he performs a ritual for safe passage and tells her how to follow mountain trails and then cross the river.

Sebastien Onius

Amabelle's lover, who works in Don Ignacio's sugar cane fields. His father was killed seven years before the story begins, in a devastating hurricane; this led him and his sister to seek work in Dominica, though his mother remains in Haiti. He is a strong, calm man, her friend and protector; when the genocide begins he disappears, presumably killed, and is never seen again. He is an enigmatic figure: intensely strong and physical, often sweaty and dirty from his hard work, but he speaks like a poet when he and Amabelle lie together in their secret cave, telling stories of his dreams and the past, of the hurricane that killed his father. He likes to talk; he dislikes silence, because "to him [it] is like sleep, a close second to death." He disappears early in the book, apparently killed by the Dominicans, but he is an almost tangible presence throughout, as Amabelle grieves and asks everyone she meets if they know what happened to him.

Papi

See Don Ignacio

Man Rapadou

Mother of Yves, who has her own secrets: when she found that her husband, a Haitian, was planning to become a spy for American interests, she cooked him a meal filled with ground glass and rat poison, and killed him. She tells Amabelle, "Greater than my love for this man was my love for my country."

Father Romain

A Haitian priest who works with the poor Haitian workers and who runs a school for their children. He often speaks of their home in Haiti, and how common language, customs, and memories bind them all together as a community. Amabelle says of him, "His creed was one of memory, how remembering—though sometimes painful—can make you strong." During the genocide, he is tortured by the Dominicans and goes insane, but eventually is healed when he leaves the priesthood, marries, and has three children. "It took more than prayers to heal me after the slaughter," he tells Amabelle. "It took a love closer to the earth, closer to my own body, to stop my tears. Perhaps I have lost, but I have also gained an ever greater understanding of things both godly and earthly."

Valencia

Daughter of Don Ignacio, wife of Pico Duarte, and mother of twin babies, a boy and a girl. She and

Amabelle grew up together, and later, during the genocide, she helps hide Haitians from the killers because she remembers how close she was to Amabelle: "I hid them because I couldn't hide you...I thought you'd been killed, so everything I did, I did in your name." She is one of the few characters in the book who does not murder, injure, or neglect someone else; despite being married to a man who carries out the orders to kill as many Haitians as possible, she works to save them.

Yves

A sugar cane worker, a refugee. Amabelle escapes with him, and not knowing where else to go, follows him to his mother's house in Haiti. They live together as if they're married, and his mother assumes they are lovers, though they are not— Amabelle is still grieving for Sebastien, who has disappeared. Yves spends long days working in his fields, only coming home at night and going to sleep immediately. He is a good man, and Amabelle regrets that they have not found more comfort in each other.

Themes

Exile

As Scott Adlerberg observed in the *Richmond Review,* "Exile increases the poignancy of memory," and many of the characters in the book are exiled, cut off from their families or homes by death or distance. Amabelle remembers her parents constantly, replaying their death by drowning in the swollen river, and talks about them with her lover Sebastien, who likewise tells her about his lost childhood in Haiti. The poor, displaced Haitians in the book all share this sense of a lost home, and it serves as a bond to unite their community—as Amabelle notes, "In his sermons to the Haitian congregants of the valley he often reminded everyone of common ties: language, foods, history, carnival, songs, tales, and prayers. His creed was one of memory, how remembering—though sometimes painful—can make you strong." The Haitian sugar cane workers consider themselves to be "an orphaned people, a group of *vwayaje,* wayfarers."

The Haitians in the book are not the only exiles; Amabelle's employer, Don Ignacio, though born in Spain, came to the Caribbean to fight in the Spanish-American War in 1898. Now, each night he scrolls up and down the radio dial to hear reports from Spain about the progress of the Spanish Civil

War. Amabelle notices his homesickness and is aware that "he felt himself the displaced child of a now orphaned people."

Despite these warnings, Amabelle, Sebastien, and the other Haitians are unprepared for the bloodbath about to occur, which will further exile those who are not slaughtered in it. The survivors, cut off from their past, those they love, and their own sense of safety and purpose, are spiritual exiles, looking for meaning and a sense of purpose; some find it, and some never do.

Genocide

The mass killing of Haitians is the central event in the book, and is described with nightmarish clarity; the book may remind readers of more recent atrocities in Bosnia and Rwanda, and the refugees flowing over the borders of these and other countries. Danticat is aware that despite the fact that events like these are visible on the news almost every night, these events seem very far away. She told Calvin Wilson in *The Kansas City Star,* "People don't want to believe that there is that kind of danger, if there is no precedent for it that they know of. They don't want to believe that, all of a sudden, thousands of people can be killed." The book is a vivid reminder that these events do happen, that they can happen to everyone, and that no one is left out of the whirlpool of death and destruction when they do occur.

Topics for Further Study

- Research the 1937 massacre of Haitians by Dominican dictator Rafael Trujillo and compare it to more recent ethnic genocides in Rwanda and Bosnia.

- Choose another dictator, such as Adolf Hitler or Haitian leader Francois "Papa Doc" Duvalier, and compare him to Rafael Trujillo. What methods did these men use to gain and keep control over their countries?

- Investigate the hurricane of 1931 and the damage it caused in Haiti and the Dominican Republic. Other than destruction of property, what long-term effects did the storm have on the economy, society, and culture of these countries?

- Consider the society you live in. Is there any evidence that a dictator like Trujillo could come to power in your own culture?

Remembrance

The themes of exile and of remembrance are related: the exiles' pain is alternately increased or soothed by their remembrance of the past. In addition, however, the book is permeated with a sense of remembrance of the actual people who suffered through these events, and the unnamed, unrecorded tens of thousands who were killed. As a man says near the end of the book, "Famous men never die...It is only those nameless and faceless who vanish like smoke in the early moning air." Danticat sees changing this fate as part of her mission as a writer, wanting to create a kind of memorial in words for all the "nameless and faceless." As Amabelle says, "All I want to do is find a place to lay it [the slaughter] down now and again, a safe nest where it will neither be scattered by the winds, nor remain forever buried beneath the sod."

The River of Death

The Massacre River, named for a mass slaughter in the seventeenth century, lives up to its name in the events of the book. Throughout the book, the river is a place of actual and symbolic death: many people die in it, corpses float down it, and once people cross it, their lives are never the same. Crossing it a second time is even harder, leading to alienation: you can never truly go back to the other side.

Amabelle's life is marked early by the river: when she is a child, her parents try to cross it to get to a market in the Dominican Republic. Though the water is visibly rising and the young boys who work carrying people and goods across refuse to go, her father insists that they enter the current. "My father reaches into the current and sprinkles his face with the water, as if to salute the spirit of the river and request her permission to cross," Amabelle says. "My mother crosses herself three times and looks up at the sky before she climbs on my father's back." Despite these ritual precautions, Amabelle's parents are swept away. Amabelle is prevented from going after them by the river boys, who drag her away, saying, "Unless you want to die, you will never see those people again."

Later, during the mass slaughter of Haitians, she and some other refugees reach the river. "From a distance," she says, "the water looked deep and black, the bank much steeper than I remembered." They hear splashing: the Dominicans are throwing corpses into the water. When they cross, they must swim to avoid the bodies and the belongings of slain Haitians: the water is literally a river of death. And when Odette, another refugee, panics because her husband has been shot while he swims across, Amabelle covers her nose and mouth to keep her quiet, "for her own good, for our own good." Odette does not struggle, but gives up to the lack of air and the motion of the river, as if she has already decided to die.

Near the end of the book, Amabelle crosses the river again, returning to the Dominican Republic, and tries to find Alegria, the region she lived in for so long. All is unrecognizable, the landmarks changed or gone, the people gone or moved, and when she finally finds her former employer Valencia, Valencia does not recognize her until she tells the story of her parents' death in the river. Valencia apologizes for this, and Amabelle tells her she understands and says she feels "like an old ghost had slipped under my skin."

Style

Pace

Danticat's story begins slowly, told with a languid, measured pace, set in a traditional agrarian society, and the first scene, after a dreamlike encounter between Amabelle and her lover Sebastien, involves the birth of twins, a boy and a girl, to her wealthy employer. At first, the book seems very much like many weighty classics of nineteenth-century literature, which begin with the birth of the protagonist.

Danticat turns this expectation upside down, however: the real hero of the story is not either of the children, but Amabelle, the servant, who midwifes them using half-remembered skills taught by her healer parents. Tinges of violence creep into the story: the twins' father kills a sugar cane worker when he runs into him with his car, but is never officially brought to justice, because the cane workers' lives are considered expendable and because he is a ranking military officer. In addition, Amabelle and Sebastien have both lost one or both parents at a young age, hinting at the precarious nature of their lives—or, as Danticat makes clear, everyone's life: no one is exempt from the possibility of violence that lurks in every person and every society.

As the story moves on, the violence escalates,

along with the pace. Rumors of an impending slaughter of Haitians begin circulating. One of the twins, the boy, dies of crib death. Haitian workers begin telling stories they've heard of other workers who were killed in recent weeks. Amabelle is almost killed by a stray bullet from her employers' target practice. And when the genocide begins, people are stabbed, shot, drowned, crushed by trucks, forced to jump off cliff, and choked with bunches of parsley—because their inability to say the word properly in Spanish marks them as Haitians.

Point of View

Throughout, Danticat's narrator Amabelle tells the story in the first person. She is there, she suffers through all these events, and Danticat's choice of this point of view, and her vivid imagery and sensory detail, gives everything an almost choking immediacy. Amabelle's narrative style is flat, almost documentary in style, as in the following paragraph:

> Her face flapped open when she hit the ground, her right cheekbone glistening as the flesh parted from it. She rolled onto her back and for a moment faced the sky. Her body spiraled past the croton hedge down the slope. The mountain dirt clung to her dress, her arms, her face, her whole body gathering a thick cloud

of dust.

Danticat deliberately avoids depicting too much emotion in the body of the book, capturing the numbness inherent to the survivors of catastrophes. Instead, she presents the scenes and allows the reader to view them and fill in the emotional impact of the slaughter, torture, and dislocation of the refugees. This participation on the reader's part makes the scenes hard to dismiss, and hard to forget. As Danticat said in an interview with Calvin Wilson in the *Kansas City Star*, "The things that I have written so far are things that almost give me nightmares."

Separation of Emotions

In the beginning and end of the book, Danticat allows Amabelle to speak more openly of her feelings in short sequences, in which she describes her dreams, her memories of her departed parents, her wishes, and her fears. These sequences are deliberately separated from the main story of the book, since Amabelle only feels safe to express them when she is alone, enclosed, in a secret cave where she hides with Sebastien, or at the end of the book, when she has reached some measure of peace with his loss and is able to come to terms with her life as a survivor apart from him. As she says, "I sense that we no longer know the same words, no longer speak the same language. There is water, land, and mountains between us, a shroud of silence, a curtain of fate."

Literary Heritage

Haiti is a country long marked by its political unrest and economic depravity as a result of years of dictatorship, government corruption, and a large gap between the wealthy elite and profitable cities and the poverty-stricken non-industrial provinces.

A written or recorded literature was never a priority in Haitian culture, therefore, the number of internationally recognized Haitian authors is understandably few. In addition, Haitian women writers are rare due to the secondary positions they hold within the society, remaining mostly in the home or in non-professional occupations.

Although fiscally poor, Haiti is a culture rich in its language, folktales, customs, and community. The Haitian people often looked to their families and friends not only for support but also for forms of entertainment. In a sense, it was the effects of poverty and illiteracy that made the practice of storytelling an important and favorite pastime, allowing this craft to endure throughout the generations, preserving the nation's culture and history.

Haitian literature was not known outside its borders until well into the 1960s, when the Civil Rights and Women's movements pushed for social reforms and gave the Haitian people an impetus to search out and explore their voices. Still, it was not until the 1990s that Haiti and Haitian literature started to receive the attention it deserved. As more and more nations began to learned of Haiti's oppression and the violence its people faced under the Duvalier government, the call for information about the country and its people increased. New emerging writers began to meet this demand, describing the horrors as well as the jewels of this besieged nation. These writers were creating a literature of social consciousness that demanded acknowledgement from the outside world. Their writing also served as a mirror in which to look back and examine their own background and culture.

When Haitian-born writer Edwidge Danticat began to write and record her memories of Haiti, fictionalizing them in her books, her writings became an extension of the oral tradition of her culture, capturing in print what was natural to her at an early age. What is present in Danticat's work is Haiti's painful history but also its uniqueness and beauty. It is this beauty and cultural lushness that are making people more open to Haitian literature and leading to changes in its presence and proliferation.

The Massacre River

In an essay in *Kreyol,* describing a 1995 visit to the river, Danticat writes, "Between Haiti and the Dominican Republic flows a river filled with ghosts." The Massacre River was named for a seventeeth-century bloodbath, but as Danticat makes clear, it has continued to live up to its name. The river divides the small Caribbean island of Hispaniola into the countries of Haiti and the Dominican Republic. Because the countries are so close, their fates have historically been intertwined. *The Farming of Bones* begins in the Republic, during the regime of General Rafael Trujillo.

Trujillo's Regime

From 1930 to 1961, the Dominican Republic was ruled by General Rafael Leonidas Trujillo, whose ascension to power was inadvertently aided by American efforts to bolster stability in the Caribbean. American leaders were interested in the Caribbean because it was a gateway to the Panama Canal, central to U.S. shipping and trade interests, and the U.S. wanted to keep the area stable and free from European intervention. Because the nations in that area were poor, politically unstable, and, in the case of the Dominican Republic, still recovering from past Spanish rule, the U.S. took over

Dominican finances, occupying the country from 1911 through 1916.

The harshness of this occupation offended Dominicans, and when the American marines left the island in 1924, they left behind an armed National Guard. Trujillo, one of the officers of the guard, used his military connections to foster a coup six years later, remove then-President Vasquez from office, and establish his own dictatorship, which lasted over three decades.

Once in office, Trujillo killed anyone opposing him and sent his thugs through the countryside, armed with machine guns, to terrorize the population. Money and ownership of land was funneled to him, resulting in widespread poverty and uprooting of entire communities. Mail was censored, telephones were monitored, and citizens needed government permission to move or practice any profession.

In 1931, a devastating hurricane struck Haiti and the Dominican Republic, killing 2,000 people and injuring many more. Trujillo used the destruction to his advantage, taking absolute power in the crisis and controlling all medicine and building supplies. He imposed "emergency" taxes, never repealed. Naturally, resentment against him grew, and he murdered, tortured, or imprisoned anyone he suspected of disloyalty.

During this period, many Haitians crossed the border into the Dominican Republic, seeking work in the wake of the devastating hurricane. Their sheer numbers began to make some Dominicans uneasy, and there was a racist tone to this unease. As the book notes, Dominicans were told, "Our motherland is Spain, theirs is darkest Africa, you understand? They once came here only to cut sugarcane, but now there are more of them than there will ever be cane to cut, you understand? Our problem is one of dominion...Those of us who love our country are taking measures to keep it our own."

Trujillo Orders Genocide

In 1937, to stop this tide of humanity and implement these "measures," Dominican troops killed between 10,000 and 15,000 Haitians. As Scott Adlerberg remarked in the *Richmond Review,* "None of those killed is anyone famous, nearly all the slaughtered are poor Haitians working as cheap labor in the neighboring country." Danticat also notes that there is often no difference in color between the two sides, despite the insistence that "our motherland is Spain, theirs is darkest Africa." Language is the only differentiating feature, and Dominican troops use the Haitians' inability to pronounce the trilled Spanish "r" in *perejil,* the word for parsley. "Que diga perejil," the soldiers demanded, and anyone who answered "pewejil" would be shot as a Haitian.

Critical Overview

Danticat is the first Haitian woman to write in English, be published by a major American press, and earn wide publicity, so she is the first one to open the door of her culture to mainstream America. Her work has received almost universally favorable reviews, and she has won numerous awards and honors for her two novels, *Breath, Eyes, Memory* and *The Farming of Bones,* and her short story collection, *Krik? Krak!*

An interesting aspect of criticism of Danticat's work is that, unlike discussions of many other writers, commentary on her work always also includes a lengthy discussion of her life, even though she is relatively young. Perhaps this is because Haiti and its culture and history are not well known to most American and European readers, so there is a certain fascination inherent in Danticat's life and in her unfamiliar culture. Perhaps it's because her first novel, *Breath, Eyes, Memory* was the semi-autobiographical story of a young girl raised by an aunt, who comes to the United States at age twelve and must deal with her family's generational issues and the dislocation of immigration to a strange place. A book like this makes readers ask about the author's life in an attempt to determine how much of the novel is "true."

Dan Cryer, who wrote one of the few

unfavorable reviews of *The Farming of Bones,* in *Salon,* seemed to be reacting to this seemingly excessive interest in Danticat's life, mainstream Americans' fascination with her "exotic" settings, and her lionization as a spokeswoman for Haitian Americans (a position that Danticat says she does not want). "Pity the young novelist surfing the wave of novelty and hype," he wrote. "Sooner or later, she's going to wipe out." Regarding the awards she's won, he asked, "A prized seat among the literati-in-waiting of *Granta* magazine's 20 Best American Novelists and a National Book Award nomination for *Krik? Krak/1* Oh, please! Has anyone actually read these books?" Cryer criticized Danticat's characterization, saying that Amabelle and Sebastien are depicted only with the broadest brush, making it "hard to care, except in the most abstract way," about their fates. "This is by far Danticat's longest book, and the stretch shows," he commented. "Only 29, Danticat has plenty of time to achieve her considerable potential. But overpraising her work won't help her get there."

Cryer seemed to be alone in his opinion, however, as other critics praised the work. "No antiseptic, nothing for the pain, just the serrated slice of her words," wrote Christopher John Farley in *Time,* "...every chapter cuts deep, and you feel it." Farley also remarked that Danticat's prose "never turns purple, never spins wildly into the fantastic, always remains focused...[and] uncovers moments of raw humanness." Scott Adlerberg, in the *Richmond Review,* praised *The Farming of Bones* as an "indelible work of art," remarking on

Danticat's "effortless style" and "simple but sensual language [that] brings her tropical world to life; one can feel the heat, see the luxuriant colors, taste the spicy foods...Amabelle is a flesh and blood woman...we share in her joys and sorrows, her dreams, memories, and day-to-day struggles." In *News-week,* Sarah Van Boven cited Danticat's beginning the book with the birth of a wealthy child, while the true hero is the servant girl Amabelle, as one of many "masterful inversions" in the book; among others, she noted, "joyful reunions turn hollow, damnation masquerades as salvation, big questions are met with a silence more profound than any answer."

As Van Boven suggests, Danticat does not provide any neat conclusion, moral lesson, or encompassing answer to the horrific events that take place in the novel. Sebastien, who is named in the first line of the book ("His name is Sebastien Onius"), soon disappears and is never seen again, and his fate is uncertain—he's presumed killed, but Amabelle, and readers, never have the satisfaction of knowing exactly what became of him. Amabelle herself, by the end of the book, is still grieving, still alone, deeply scarred by the genocide—and she always will be. Nothing in the book is predictable except that inevitably, pain and sorrow will enter everyone's life. A *Publishers Weekly* reviewer noted that when violence does erupt in the book, the story develops the "unflinching clarity" of a documentary. The review also praised Danticat's realistic characterizations, the dignity of the people described, and her "lushly poetic and erotic, specifically detailed" prose. Calvin Wilson, in *The Kansas City Star,* wrote, "There's little doubt that, at a time when some writers gain attention simply by emphasizing the glib, the trendy and the superficial, Danticat will continue to create works of enduring weight."

What Do I Read Next?

- Danticat's *Krik? Krakl* is a collection of short stories set in Haiti. The title comes from a traditional Haitian custom of listeners asking "Krik?" before a story is told. The teller answers "Krak" and begins the tale.

- *Breath, Eyes, Memory,* also by Danticat, tells the story of a twelve-year-old Haitian girl, raised by an aunt, who comes to the United States and is reunited with her mother for the first time since infancy.

- *Trujillo: The Death of the Dictator,* by Bernard Diederich, documents Trujillo's ascension to power, rule over the Dominican Republic, and assassination.

- Philip Gourevitch's *We Regret to Inform You That Tomorrow We Will Be Killed with Our Families* is a collection of harrowing first-person accounts of the genocide in Rwanda.

Sources

Adlerberg, Scott, "The Farming of Bones," in *Richmond Review* (online), 2000.

Charters, Mallay, "Edwidge Danticat: A Bitter Legacy Revisited," in *Publishers Weekly,* August 17, 1998, p. 42.

Cryer, Dan, "The Farming of Bones," in *Salon* (online).

Danticat, Edwidge, "A Brief Reflection on the Massacre River," in *Kreyol* (online), May 19, 1999.

"The Farming of Bones," in *Publishers Weekly,* June 8, 1998, p. 44.

Rooney, Megan, "Danticat MFA '94 Reads from *The Farming of Bones,'*" in *Brown Daily Herald,* October 5, 1998.

Van Boven, Sarah, "Massacre River: Danticat Revisits Haiti," in *Newsweek,* September 7, 1998, p. 69.

Wilson, Calvin, "Edwidge Danticat's Prose Floats in Realm of Sadness and Eloquence," in *Kansas City Star,* September 22, 1999, p. K0779.

Further Reading

Acosta, Belinda "The Farming of Bones," *in Austin Chronicle,* January 19, 1999.

> This discussion of Danticat's book also has comments about her writing in general.

Brice-Finch, Jacqueline, "Haiti," in *World Literature Today,* Spring, 1999, p. 373.

> Brief review of *The Farming of Bones* in the context of Haitian history.

Farley, Christopher John, "The Farming of Bones," in *Time,* September 7, 1998, p. 78.

> Farley discusses Danticat's writing career and her books.

Gardiner, Beth, "Writer's Work Evokes Experience of Haitian Regime, Emigration," in *Standard-Times,* April 12,1998.

> Explores Danticat's experiences in Haiti and how they fuel her fiction.

Gladstone, Jim, "Breath, Eyes, Memory," in *New York Times Book Review,* July 10, 1994, p. 24.

> Brief review of the book.

Jaffe, Zia, "The Farming of Bones," in *The Nation,* November 16, 1998, p. 62.

Brief review.

Shea, Renee H., "An Interview between Edwidge Danticat and Renee H. Shea," in *Belles Lettres,* Summer, 1995, pp. 12-15.

> Shea and Danticat discuss her life and works.